Piano Solos of ...

MW01259278

10 Arrangements for Preludes, Offertories and Postludes

Arranged by **Jan Sanborn**

Although the choral repertoire is filled with many beautiful standards, the pianist is often relegated to undertake a subordinate role in their performance. While accompanying has its rewards, why not arrange some of these elegant and beloved pieces for solo piano? Some of them, like "Jesu, Joy of Man's Desiring" by Johann Sebastian Bach and "Cantique" by Gabriel Fauré, almost play themselves. The existing choral accompaniments are flowing and the melodies are distinct. Others require more creative arranging, such as including some extensions or other enhancements, to make them more pianistic and interesting to the listener. John Stainer's "God So Loved the World" is such a piece, lending itself to an arpeggiated underscoring of its beautiful melody. Paul Tschesnokoff's "May Thy Holy Spirit" challenges one to approximate the deep resonance of the bass lines and, at the same time, to create harmonic and melodic interest. Similar considerations are apparent in Peter Lutkin's "The Lord Bless You and Keep You." There was a different sort of challenge in "Sing to God," which is homophonic in character but with many vocal entrances that need to be observed and brought out.

It is my hope and desire that pianists will enjoy learning and performing these "choral piano pieces," bringing new awareness of these choral masterworks' beauty and significance in music literature.

Jan Sanborn

Alfred Music Publishing Co., Inc.
P.O. Box 10003
Van Nuys, CA 91410-0003
alfred.com

ISBN-10: 0-7390-7347-8
ISBN-13: 978-0-7390-7347-6

Cover Photo
The choir stalls of San Marcos: © shutterstock.com / Alvaro German Vilela

God So Loved the World

John Stainer

Arr. Jan Sanborn

Freely, tenderly ($\quarternote$ = 88)

pedal lightly

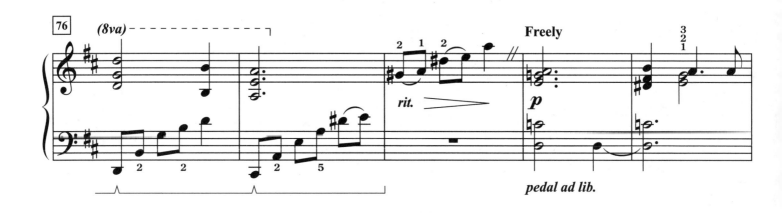

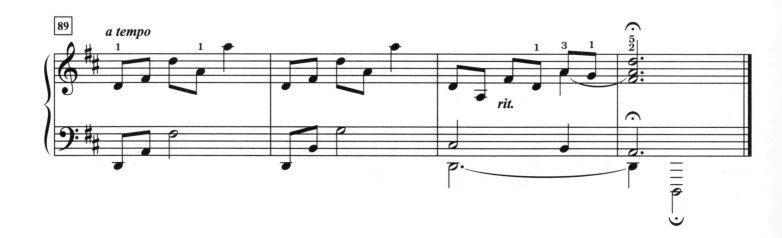

(Approx. Performance Time—2:30)

Jesu, Joy of Man's Desiring

Johann Sebastian Bach

Arr. Jan Sanborn

Ave Verum

Wolfgang Amadeus Mozart
Arr. Jan Sanborn

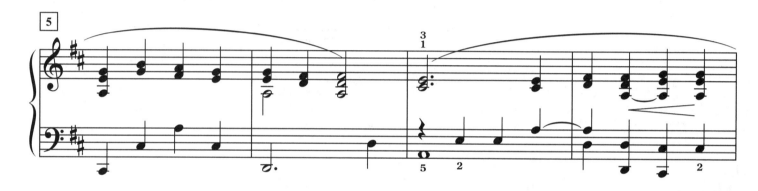

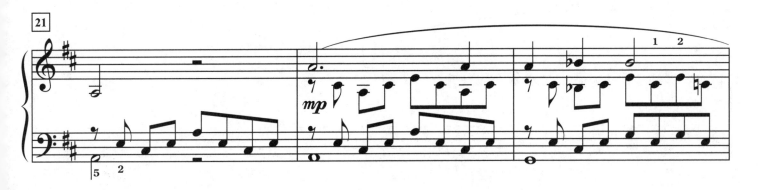

(Approx. Performance Time—3:00)

Sanctus

Gabriel Fauré

Arr. Jan Sanborn

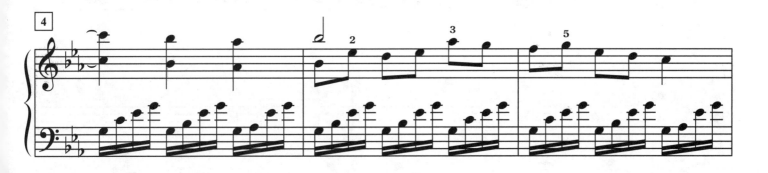

14

(Approx. Performance Time—2:30)

May Thy Holy Spirit

Paul Tschesnokoff

Arr. Jan Sanborn

Più mosso

Tempo I

Cast Thy Burden Upon the Lord

Felix Mendelssohn

Arr. Jan Sanborn

(Approx. Performance Time—4:00)

Cantique

Gabriel Fauré
Arr. Jan Sanborn

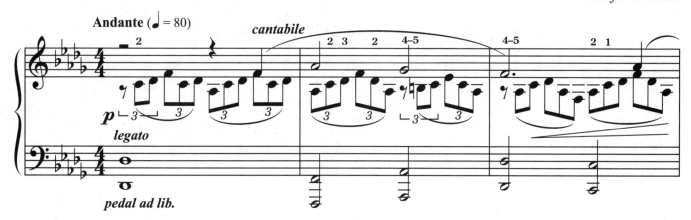

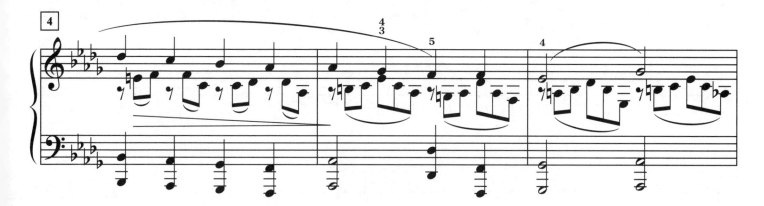

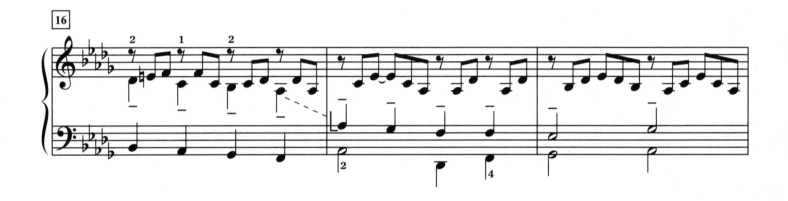

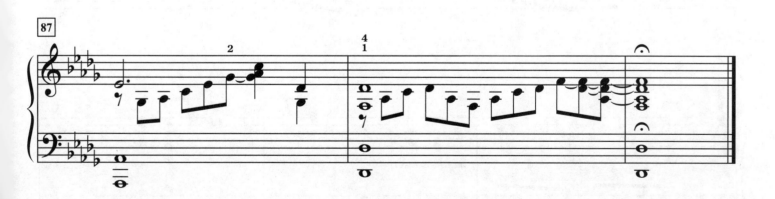

Sing to God

George Frideric Handel

Arr. Jan Sanborn

(Approx. Performance Time—4:00)

He, Watching Over Israel

Felix Mendelssohn
Arr. Jan Sanborn

The Lord Bless You and Keep You

Peter C. Lutkin

Arr. Jan Sanborn

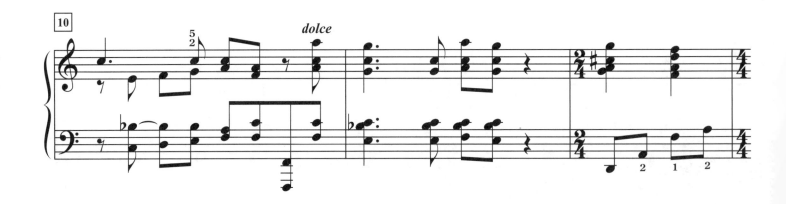